DOPAMINE AND SUCCESS

Utilizing Dopamine Detox for Lesser Distractions, Greater Focus, and Ultimate Achievement

James Edwards

All rights reserved. No part of this publication may be reproduced, distributed, or transmitted in any form or by any means, including photocopying, recording, or other electronic or mechanical methods, without the prior written permission of the publisher, except in the case of brief quotations embodied in critical reviews and certain other noncommercial uses permitted by copyright law.

Copyright © by James Edwards 2024

TABLE OF CONTENTS

INTRODUCTION

CHAPTER ONE

Basic Knowledge and Effects of Dopamine

CHAPTER TWO

Mastering Dopamine Detox

CHAPTER THREE

How to Prepare for Dopamine Detox

CHAPTER FOUR

Recognizing Digital Distractions

CHAPTER FIVE

Three Principal Approaches to Digital Detoxification

CHAPTER SIX

Understanding the Scientific Foundation of the Character of Focus

CHAPTER SEVEN

Three Powerful Methods for Mastering Productivity Techniques

CHAPTER EIGHT

How to Get the Best Sleep for Productivity

CHAPTER NINE

Maintaining the Mind and Body

CHAPTER TEN

Conquering the Three Main Obstacles on the Path to Dopamine Detox

CHAPTER ELEVEN

How to Include Dopamine Detox in Your Lifestyle in Three Easy Steps

CONCLUSION

ABOUT THE AUTHOR

INTRODUCTION

It can seem impossible to regain our focus and accomplish our goals in a world full of nonstop stimuli and distractions. This book serves as guidance for overcoming the attention overload environment of this recent era, providing useful neuroscientific tactics to assist you in escaping the hindrances of distraction and maximizing the benefits of intentional, focused living.

This book examines how our digital age has taken over our dopamine systems, resulting in severe distraction and decreased productivity. It does this examination by employing the most recent research on dopamine, which is the brain's reward molecule that is essential to motivation and pleasure. We explore practical methods to regulate our habits, retrain our brains, and take back control of our attention, utilizing dopamine detox mastery.

This book offers a blueprint to realizing your maximum potential, whether you're a student aiming for academic distinction, an entrepreneur pursuing immense success, or just someone hoping to live a more purposeful life. Come along on a voyage of self-discovery and metamorphosis as we reveal the secrets to fewer distractions, sharper focus, and eventually, realizing your most daring ambitions.

CHAPTER ONE

Basic Knowledge and Effects of Dopamine

Dopamine is a chemical messenger in the brain nerves that is essential for motivation and pleasure. It is frequently referred to as the brain's reward molecule. Its connection to compulsive habits, difficulty concentrating, and present-day distractions have come under close investigation in recent years, which has sparked an increased interest in dopamine detoxification techniques as a means of improving general success, regaining focus, and minimizing distractions.

Four Major Functions of Dopamine in the Brain

The brain produces dopamine in a number of areas, including the ventral tegmental area and the substantia nigra. It influences several different mental and emotional processes through a variety of functions:

1. Pleasure and Reward: Dopamine and the brain's reinforcement are intimately related. When we achieve something worthwhile — whether it's finishing a task, reaching a goal, or having a pleasurable experience — it reinforces behaviors by giving us a sensation of pleasure.

2. Motivation: Dopamine is a key neurotransmitter that propels us to act to satisfy our cravings and seek our objectives. When we're doing things that are in line with our interests and objectives, it's what gives us energy and focus.

3. Memory and Learning: Dopamine helps people learn by fortifying the brain pathways linked to pleasurable experiences. It assists us in recalling the behaviors that produce favorable results, directing our future actions and choices.

4. Motor Control: Dopamine is essential for both mental and body balance control processes, coordinating movement and maintaining smooth muscles coordinated functions.

Four Major Negative Effects of Undue Dopamine Stimulation

Although dopamine is necessary for normal brain function, too much stimulation can be harmful:

1. Addictive Behaviors: Addiction can result from overabundant dopamine release, which is frequently brought on by substances or behaviors that are addictive, such as playing video games and gambling. These behaviors take over the brain's reinforcement, starting a vicious cycle where one must keep chasing rewards to feel the same amount of pleasure.

2. Recklessness: Recklessness and risk-taking behaviors may be influenced by elevated dopamine levels. This may show up as having trouble focusing, acting rashly, or wanting satisfaction right now.

3. Anxiety and Stress: Severe stress and anxiety disorders can both be influenced by undue dopamine release. Anxiety and discontent can get out of control when rewards are constantly sought after or when one fears they won't be obtained.

4. Attention Impairment: Individuals with attention impairment disorders, such as Attention-Deficit Hyperactivity Disorder, battle with focus, organization, and delayed gratification. Dopamine imbalance is connected to these conditions.

The Function of Dopamine in Fueling Present-Day Distractions

Dopamine is a major factor in the current distractions that are prevalent in today's hyperlinked world of social media, notifications, and continual stimulation:

1. Social Media and Dopamine: Likes, comments, and alerts on social media sites are intended to cause the release of dopamine. An inability to focus on crucial activities and obsessive usage behaviors might result from this never-ending response cycle.

2. Multitasking and Dopamine: Although it is frequently believed that multitasking increases productivity, it actually impairs performance and focus. Dopamine is released when you switch between things, yet your brain finds it difficult to focus deeply on one thing at a time.

3. Instant Gratification: Our brains are wired to seek out benefits right now because of the widespread availability of freelance services and fast information access. This need for rapid satisfaction has the potential to thwart long-term objectives that need consistent work and attention.

In conclusion, anyone looking to increase attention, lessen distractions, and successfully accomplish their goals must comprehend the function of dopamine in the brain, how it affects behavior, and how it relates to present-day distractions. People can take back control of their dopamine response, develop better habits, and feel more fulfilled in life by putting techniques like dopamine detox into practice.

CHAPTER TWO

Mastering Dopamine Detox

The phrase 'Dopamine Detox' has become quite popular in the fields of success and personal growth in the last few years. However, what is dopamine detoxification precisely, and how might it improve our ability to focus and work more efficiently? In order to comprehend this, we must investigate the concept's origins and development, examine its advantages, and debunk myths and misunderstandings.

The Origin and Development of Dopamine Detox

Dopamine detoxification has its origins in archaic ideologies that place a strong importance on temperance, self-control, and discipline. It was once thought that rituals like meditation, fasting, and purposeful abstinence from particular pleasures would improve resilience, develop the mind, and increase self-awareness.

Dopamine detoxification has been impacted by psychology and neuroscience in the modern era. Often referred to as the "reward neurotransmitter," dopamine is essential for pleasure, motivation, and feedback-based learning. Decreased responsiveness to natural rewards can result from overstimulating the dopamine system, which is mostly caused by marathon viewing of television shows, scrolling through social media, and consuming sweet or fatty foods all the time.

Dopamine detox is not about getting rid of dopamine; rather, it's about resetting the release of dopamine through less exposure to intensely stimulating activities and more intentional breaks, introspection, and participation in relevant projects.

The Top Five Advantages of Dopamine Detox

1. Less Distractions: People can reclaim power over their focus and lessen distractions by purposefully reducing their vulnerability to instant gratification sources like social media and video games.

2. Increased Focus: Reading, learning, and artistic endeavors are among the activities that people who are on a dopamine detox are more likely to undertake because they need continuous attention and intense concentration.

3. Increased Productivity: Productivity naturally rises when focus is sharpened and distractions are minimized. Dopamine detoxification facilitates goal-setting, task prioritization, and advancement toward established goals.

4. Better Mental Health: Prolonged engagement in mentally taxing activities can exacerbate stress, anxiety, and exhaustion. Dopamine detoxification gives people a break, enabling them to recover emotionally and cognitively.

5. Enhanced Self-awareness: People can better understand their habits, motives, and values by retreating from routine activities and considering their effects. For one to improve and progress personally, self-awareness is essential.

Four Major Misconceptions and Myths Surrounding Dopamine Detox

1. Dopamine Elimination: In contrast to what many people think, the goal of dopamine detoxification is not to completely remove dopamine or bring about a life of joyless self-denial. Rather, the aim is to realign the brain's reward system to enhance responsiveness to significant events.

2. Immediate Results: Dopamine detoxification is a long procedure that calls for dedication and persistence rather than a speedy cure. Even though some people could benefit right away, long-lasting changes usually take time to manifest.

3. Equal for Everyone: There isn't a dopamine detox strategy that works for everyone. Based on personal preferences, objectives, and lifestyle variables, different strategies may be used. To determine what works best, flexibility and testing are essential.

4. Total Abstinence: Total abstinence from pleasurable activities is not required during a dopamine detox. Rather, it promotes restraint and sensible consumption, guaranteeing that pleasures continue to be fulfilling and significant.

In summary, the idea of dopamine detox provides a useful basis for overcoming the obstacles of contemporary living and promoting increased fulfillment, attention, and resilience. Through knowledge of its origin, acceptance of its advantages, and debunking of myths, people can use dopamine detoxification to achieve their goals and advance personally.

CHAPTER THREE

How to Prepare for Dopamine Detox

The first step in any dopamine detox is preparation. This chapter explores the vital processes of evaluating your existing routines and habits, establishing specific intentions and goals, and establishing a nurturing atmosphere. These measures set the stage for an effective dopamine detoxification, which reduces distractions, increases focus, and ultimately results in greater success.

Four Methods for Evaluating Present Routines and Habits for Dopamine Detox

It is important to have a firm grasp of your present routines and behaviors before beginning a dopamine detox. Examining how you utilize your time, endeavors that make you happy or stressed, and recognizing any patterns that might be causing undue dopamine stimulation are all part of this self-analyzing process.

1. Time Audit: Start by carrying out a complete time audit. For a minimum of one week, keep a journal of your daily activities. Make a note of everything you do, including using social media, playing video games, streaming, working on projects, working out, unwinding, and sleeping.

2. Emotional Monitor: Consider your feelings both before and after each task. Do some tasks give you a sense of fulfillment and energy, or do they make it difficult for you to concentrate and stay motivated? Concentrate on tasks that elicit addiction or impulsive actions.

3. Determine Triggers: Determine what sets off actions that are meant to produce the brain reward effect of dopamine. These triggers could be particular settings, social media alerts, stress, or restlessness. Being aware of your triggers enables you to prepare for and control them during the detoxification process.

4. Analyze Productivity: Determine how productive you were at various tasks. Ascertain which of your tasks are wreckers or distractions and which ones help you achieve your goals.

Four Steps to Establishing Explicit Goals and Intentions for Dopamine Detox

It's time to establish specific objectives and ambitions for your dopamine detox after you've taken a thorough inventory of your present routines. Setting goals helps you stay motivated and focused while working toward significant change.

1. Specify Goals: Make sure you know exactly what you want to get out of the dopamine detox. Your goals can be to cut back on screen time, increase productivity and focus, develop better habits, or take back your free time to engage in relevant pursuits.

2. SMART Goals: To organize your goals for effectiveness, utilize the SMART standards to establish them. SMART is an acronym, where S stands for Specific, M stands for Measurable, A stands for Achievable, R stands for Relevant, and T stands for Time-bound. For instance, designate particular hours for concentrated work free from interruptions or make a goal to cut down on daily screen usage by thirty percent in the following month.

3. Prioritize Your Goals: Sort your objectives according to how important they are to your general productivity and success. Take it one at a time, prioritize one or two main objectives at first to prevent feeling overburdened.

4. Visualize Success: Envision yourself attaining your objectives and reaping the rewards of a dopamine response that is in harmony. All through the detox process, use mental image practices to reaffirm your commitment and maintain your motivation.

Four Strategies to Establish a Dopamine Detox Supportive Environment

In the course of a dopamine detox, maintaining beneficial improvements requires a supportive environment. Make sure everything around you promotes motivation, focus, and success.

1. Sort Out Physical Space: To lessen distractions and foster tranquility, organize your physical surroundings. Sort out your work area, clear out useless items, and establish a comfortable environment for concentrated work or leisure.

2. Restrict Temptations: Recognize and restrict the temptations that could undermine your attempts to detox. This may include limiting the amount of time you spend on apps, obstructing disturbing websites, or designating some areas of your house as tech-free.

3. Create a Support System: Ask friends, family, or online groups for help if you need it. These people will know your objectives and will be there to cheer you on when things get tough. Talk about your progress, acknowledge your successes, and ask for help when necessary.

4. Prioritize Self-Care: Give self-care tasks like consistent exercise, enough sleep, mindfulness exercises, and a balanced diet top priority. A healthy body and mind are more suitable to withstand the difficulties of a dopamine detox.

You create a strong basis for a dopamine detox that works by carefully evaluating your routines, establishing specific goals, and creating a nurturing atmosphere. In the upcoming chapters, we'll look at useful tactics and methods for carrying out your detox plan in a way that will minimize distractions, improve focus, and help you achieve great success.

CHAPTER FOUR

Recognizing Digital Distractions

Digital distractions have become very common in the present-day world, consuming our focus at every turn and permeating every part of our lives. Our digital environment is made to fascinate and enthrall us, from the seduction of social media to the never-ending supply of entertainment alternatives and the incessant assault of emails and messages. But there is a price to this ceaseless incitement, and it frequently results in a loss of focus, reduced performance, and a feeling of exhaustion. We'll explore several types of digital distractions in this chapter, such as the constant barrage of emails and notifications, digital entertainment habits, and social media distractions.

Four Primary Signs to Warn of Social Media Distraction

Social media platforms have completely changed the way we relate and interact, enabling us to keep in touch with our loved ones and the rest of the world. But social media's seductive qualities can quickly result in overuse and distraction. The following four indicators are the main ones that indicate you might be getting distracted by social media:

1. Excessive Time Spent: Do you often lose sense of time while browsing social media feeds for hours at once?

2. Constant Checking: Do you feel pressured to review your social media accounts frequently throughout the day, even when you have essential things to complete?

3. Fear of Missing Out: Do you frequently experience anxiety or jealousy after viewing the posts of others, which then causes you to feel as though you're missing out?

4. Effect on Productivity: Have you found that using social media too much has made you less productive, taking longer to accomplish chores or leaving them undone?

Four Signs of Unhealthy Digital Entertainment Habits

Since it promotes happiness and relaxation, entertainment is an essential aspect of existence. Digital entertainment can, nevertheless, make it more difficult for us to concentrate and accomplish our objectives if it starts to operate as a continual source of distraction. Four signs of unhealthy digital entertainment habits are as follows:

1. Marathon Watching of a TV Show: Do you often find yourself putting off other obligations in order to watch TV series or movies nonstop for long periods of time?

2. Addiction to Playing Video Games: Do video games take up a large amount of your time, interfering with your regular activities and commitments?

3. Mindless Internet Browsing: Do you frequently jump aimlessly between websites while browsing the web?

4. Ignoring Essential Activities: Have your digital entertainment habits caused you to overlook essential activities like exercise, social relations, or recreation?

Four Warning Signs of Distractions from Email and Notifications

In the current digital era, the constant barrage of emails, messages, and notifications has emerged as a significant cause of distraction. Although it's crucial to keep in touch, the ceaseless alerts, sounds, and notifications can cause us to lose focus and become less productive. The following four warning signs suggest that you might be getting distracted by emails and notifications:

1. Immediate Response Syndrome: Despite the fact that an email or message is not urgent, do you still feel obligated to answer it right away?

2. Notification Distractions: Do you frequently experience disturbance from your devices as a result of the alerts from different apps buzzing nonstop?

3. Email Plague: Is it difficult for you to select and efficiently handle your communications because your inbox is flooded with unread emails?

4. Simultaneous Execution of Multiple Tasks Problem: Do you frequently find yourself trying to do too many things at once because there are always delays?

To successfully perform a dopamine detox, the first step is to recognize these digital distractions. By acknowledging the habits and actions that lead to your inability to concentrate, you can start to recover your focus and direct it towards worthwhile endeavors. We will look at methods and approaches in the upcoming chapters to assist you overcome these distractions, improve your concentration, and eventually reach your objectives with direction and certainty.

CHAPTER FIVE

Three Principal Approaches to Digital Detoxification

Developing techniques for digital detoxification has become essential in this era of perpetual connectivity in order to preserve mental health, minimize distractions, and promote improved focus. In order to create a better connection with technology, this chapter examines three key strategies: setting screen time restrictions, engaging in sensible social media usage, and adopting disconnecting methods.

1. Setting Screen Time Restrictions: Limiting the amount of time you spend on your devices' screens is one of the best methods to begin a digital detox. Start by calculating the amount of time you now spend using viewing screens on a daily basis, such as computers, televisions, tablets, and cellphones. These days, a lot of gadgets come with built-in capabilities for tracking screen time and establishing limits.

Begin by setting up specified time slots for various pursuits, including work, play, and private moments. When you hit your daily screen time limit, utilize software or facilities that let you oblige these restrictions by locking your smartphone automatically or sending you notifications. Reduce the amount of time you spend on screens gradually to establish a long-lasting habit.

2. Sensible Use of Social Media: While social media can foster connections, it can also lead to possible distractions and addictive habits. By using social media with awareness, you may maximize its positive effects while reducing its detrimental effects on your concentration and performance.

Fundamentally, purge accounts on social media that don't support your ideals or make a positive difference in your life. This will help you manage your social media feeds. Instead of continuously browsing through social media all through the day, set aside particular periods to check it. Make learned judgments towards your digital consumption by using apps that monitor your social media activity and offer enlightenment into your patterns of using them.

Be totally present when utilizing social media as another way to engage in digital consciousness. Pay attention to one task at a time and make plans for your online communications to abstain from multitasking or aimless browsing. Instead of casually reading through content, actively engage with it to understand it deeply and lessen the need to check for updates all the time.

3. Unplugging Techniques: Even for brief periods of time, turning off all digital devices can have a positive impact on your general success and mental health. Include unplugging strategies in your everyday routine to take short breaks from technology and re-establish your connection to the outside world.

Establish designated areas in your house, like the eating place or bedroom, where electronics are not permitted. Initiate consistent "digital detox" days where you give up using any electronics and instead engage in creative and calming pursuits like reading, journaling, or hanging around outside.

To control digital addictions and lessen anxiety connected to overuse, try mindfulness exercises or meditation. Utilize features on your gadgets, such as warning signs to refrain from disturbance, to establish uninterrupted times for engrossment and attention.

You may develop a wiser attachment to technology, cut down on distractions, improve your focus, and ultimately reach higher levels of performance and achievement in your private and business life by putting these digital detox ideas into practice.

CHAPTER SIX

Understanding the Scientific Foundation of the Character of Focus

Mastering the science initiating focus, neuroplasticity, and the variables affecting concentration is crucial as we work to perfect focus and accomplish our goals. By exploring these areas, we can find effective methods for enhancing focus and realizing our full potential.

The Relationship Between Focus and Neuroplasticity

Our capacity for focus is greatly influenced by neuroplasticity, the brain's capacity to rearrange itself during life by creating new neural connections. Our experiences, our thoughts, and the skills we develop all have an impact on the shape and functionality of the brain.

Specific areas in the brain play a major role in focus. The thalamus serves as a booster for sensory information, and it works closely with the prefrontal cortex, which is in charge of higher-order mental processes including focus and decision-making. By reducing distractions and processing pertinent information, they work together to control focus.

Furthermore, dopamine neurotransmitters are essential for the process of focus. Dopamine is frequently referred to as the "motivation molecule" because of its effects on focus, drive, and reward-seeking habits. Comprehending the ways in which dopamine levels alter in reaction to various stimuli might aid us in managing our focus and performance.

Four Principal Factors That May Influence Our Focus

Our capacity to focus can be impacted by a number of things, such as:

1. Environmental Distractions: Noisy environments, cluttered workstations, and electronic distractions can all cause us to lose focus and distract our attention. Establishing a well-structured and comfortable environment is crucial for encouraging focus.

2. Emotional State: Our feelings have a big impact on how focused we are. While happy emotions can improve mental function, stress, worry, and negative emotions can usurp our focus. These emotional states can be controlled with the use of emotional management and mindfulness practices.

3. Sleep and Physical Health: A healthy diet, consistent exercise, and enough sleep are all essential for mental performance. Fatigue, mental haze, and decreased focus can result from an inability to sleep and unhealthy lifestyle choices.

4. Multitasking: Despite what the general public believes, multitasking frequently lowers productivity and impedes focus. Because of the limitations of our brains, multitasking causes mistakes and lowers performance.

Six Effective Techniques to Sharpen Your Focus

There are a number of tactics we can use to maximize focus and perform at our best, including:

1. Mindfulness and Meditation: Mindfulness training increases concentration, decreases daydreaming, and fosters awareness of the here and now. Frequent meditation strengthens the brain circuits linked to emotional control and focus.

2. Pomodoro Technique: This technique for managing your time entails working in concentrated bursts (like twenty-five minutes) interspersed with brief pauses. It increases productivity by taking advantage of the brain's innate pattern of focus and relaxation.

3. Digital Detox: You can reduce digital distractions and encourage lasting focus by setting limits on screen usage, turning off notifications, and setting aside specific times for in-depth work.

4. Prioritization and Goal Setting: Stating goals with clarity, dividing work into digestible chunks, and giving productive activities priority help to create precision and purpose, which clears the mind and improves focus.

5. Optimizing Environment: You may make a workspace that is ideal for focus by keeping it clutter-free, reducing noise, and adding relaxing aspects like plants and natural light.

6. Physical Health Habits: Getting enough rest, exercising frequently, and eating a diet high in nutrients that strengthen the brain are all important for maintaining focus and mental performance.

By incorporating these scientific discoveries into our everyday routines and implementing focused tactics, we may start a dopamine detox, reduce distractions, improve focus, and realize our greatest potential for success.

CHAPTER SEVEN

Three Powerful Methods for Mastering Productivity Techniques

Learning productivity strategies is essential if we are to realize our full potential and produce outstanding outcomes. We'll explore three powerful methods for utilizing productive strategies in this chapter, and they include Time Blocking and the Pomodoro Technique, Prioritization, and Task Management, and Mindfulness and Meditation Practices. We may develop a route to topmost achievement, reduce distractions, and unleash higher focus by incorporating these tactics into our daily habits.

1. Time Blocking and Pomodoro Technique: One powerful method for efficiently organizing your agenda is time blocking. The idea is straightforward: organize your day into discrete time slots for different kinds of work or chores. Establishing time blocks for tasks like communication via email, job tasks, and personal growth helps to establish an organized environment that promotes efficiency.

In addition to time blocking, Francesco Cirillo's Pomodoro Technique improves focus and helps people avoid procrastination. The technique calls for twenty-five minutes of serious work termed a "Pomodoro", interspersed with five-minute breaks. Once you've finished four sessions of such work or four Pomodoros, take a lengthier break of between fifteen to thirty minutes. This disciplined rhythm makes the most of focused work cycles and restorative breaks to maximize productivity.

The following four stages should be followed in order to successfully use Time Blocking and the Pomodoro Technique:

a. Schedule Your Day: Depending on your energy level and priorities, set up certain time slots for important chores.

b. Establish Specific Goals: To keep focus and motivation high, establish specific goals for every time block or Pomodoro session.

c. Remove Distractions: Reduce disturbances during work cycles by turning off notifications and setting up a comfortable environment.

d. Review and Modify: To maximize performance, periodically evaluate your production levels and modify time blocks or Pomodoro lengths as necessary.

2. Prioritization and Task Management: The foundation of efficient task management is prioritization. It entails determining which tasks will have the greatest influence and importance and allocating resources appropriately. Tasks can be prioritized according to their urgency, relevance, and agreement with ultimate goals to make sure your actions are focused on valuable tasks.

The following are four essential methods for managing tasks and setting priorities:

a. Eisenhower Matrix: Utilize this matrix to divide jobs into the following four groups: neither important nor urgent, urgent but not important, important but not urgent, and both important and urgent. To increase productivity, concentrate on the tasks that are both important and urgent, as well as, the tasks that are important but not urgent.

b. ABCDE Method: Give tasks a priority (A, B, or C) according to their importance. Tasks A through C are essential, B is significant but less urgent, and C is optional or transferable.

c. Task batching: Assemble related jobs in a group to simplify workflow and reduce interchanging work contexts which can affect productivity negatively.

d. Regular Reviews: change your task list on a consistent basis to make sure it is in line with overall objectives, assign tasks as needed, and constantly review your priorities.

3. Mindfulness and Meditation Practices: These two powerful techniques can improve focus, lower stress levels, and develop a calm, clear mentality that is helpful for productivity. Practicing mindfulness on a regular basis can greatly enhance your capacity to control distractions and maintain present-moment awareness.

Here are four realistic strategies to incorporate mindfulness and meditation into your daily habits to increase productivity:

a. Morning Mindfulness: To improve focus and create a happy atmosphere, begin your day with a quick mindfulness exercise like deep breathing, meditation, or gratitude journaling.

b. Mindful Work Sessions: All through work sessions, cultivate mindful awareness by giving your whole attention to the task at hand. To buttress your concentration, try deep breathing exercises.

c. Mindful Breaks: All through the day, take consistent pauses to refresh and refocus. To refresh your mind and body, utilize these pauses for quick meditation sessions, stretches, or mindful walks.

d. Evening Reflection: Express your thoughts for the day by writing in a notebook or engaging in a thankfulness activity as a way to reflect on your day. Determine accomplishments, opportunities for development, and lessons gained to raise performance and self-awareness.

You may engage the skill of dopamine detox to reduce distractions, increase focus, and accomplish your goals by incorporating these productivity tactics into your daily habits with an emphasis on consistency and flexibility.

CHAPTER EIGHT

How to Get the Best Sleep for Productivity

One of the fundamental anchors in our quest for increased success, productivity, and focus is sound sleep, which is sometimes disregarded. Before delving into the details of dopamine detoxification and mental focus, it is important to realize how much sleep optimization affects our general health and concentration. This chapter will cover the value of getting a good night's sleep, practical sleep hygiene tips, and methods for dealing with common sleep disorders like insomnia and restlessness.

The Value of Good Sleep

The intensity and rejuvenating qualities of sleep are equally as important as the number of hours used up in bed when determining the soundness of sleep. Our bodies go through vital functions including hormone balance, memory rationalization, and cell regeneration when we sleep. These processes are hampered by insufficient and unrestful sleep, which can result in reduced mental performance, emotional swings, and a general deterioration of psychological and biological health.

Studies have indicated that humans generally benefit from seven to nine hours of sleep every night. Personal needs, however, could differ, and variables including age, degree of activity, and health issues might affect how much sleep a person needs. Prioritizing steadiness in sleep routines is crucial, with the goal of achieving sufficient length and quality of sleep.

Six Crucial Sleep Hygiene Habits

A collection of routines and behaviors that support sound sleep patterns is referred to as sleep hygiene. Through the integration of these techniques into our everyday lives, we can establish a setting that promotes healthy and revitalizing sleep. These are the following six crucial sleep hygiene habits:

1. Maintain a Regular Sleep Schedule: Your physiological circadian rhythm or body's internal clock is regulated when you go to bed and wake up simultaneously every day, including weekends. The practice of going to sleep at a steady moment every day will therefore improve the standard of your sleep.

2. Establish a Calm Bedtime Routine: Read, meditate, or take a warm bath as a restful activity before bed. Steer clear of energizing activities that can interfere with your sleep, such as viewing the television or making use of electronics that emit blue light.

3. Create An Ideal Sleep Environment: Endeavor that your bedroom is cool, quiet, and dark. Acquire a cozy mattress and pillows that promote good sleep and body position.

4. Limit Alcohol and Caffeine: Steer clear of ingesting alcohol or caffeine right before bed because they might cause your sleep rhythm to be disturbed and hamper your ability to fall asleep.

5. Frequent Exercise: Getting frequent exercise in the day will help you get better sleep. Abstain from engaging in strenuous exercise too soon before bed, though, as it may be arousing.

6. Mindfulness and Stress Control: To lower stress and encourage unwinding before bed, try mindfulness meditation, yoga, or deep breathing exercises.

Five Methods for Dealing with Restlessness and Insomnia

Many people may however suffer from restlessness and insomnia occasionally or chronically irrespective of observing sleep hygiene practices. These sleep disorders can have a serious negative effect on our general health and day-to-day activities. Here are five methods for dealing with restlessness and insomnia:

1. Determine the Root Causes: Investigate any possible root causes of your sleep problems, such as stress, worry, depression, or sleep abnormalities. Effective treatment must deal with these underlying issues.

2. Cognitive Behavioral Therapy for Insomnia (CBT-I): The goal of CBT-I, a very successful treatment, is to alter unfavorable thought practices and habits linked to sleep problems. It places a strong emphasis on mental programming, sleep limitation, and calming methods to enhance the quality of sleep.

3. Sleep Supplements and Drugs: To assist in treating insomnia, medical professionals may suggest sleeping supplements or drugs. These can have negative consequences by increasing the danger of dependency, thus they should only be used sparingly and under expert supervision.

4. Lifestyle Modifications: Consider whether your lifestyle choices — such as too much screen time, inconsistent sleep schedules, or unsuitable sleeping conditions — may be aggravating your sleep issues. Make consistent modifications to make these aspects better.

5. Speak with a Healthcare Provider: If self-care measures are ineffective in addressing sleep disruptions, consider consulting a medical practitioner or sleep specialist for advice. They are able to carry out an exhaustive assessment, provide suitable therapies, and track advancement in the course of time.

We may maximize our refreshing sleep and improve our mental functions, focus, and productivity by emphasizing high-quality sleep and putting good sleep hygiene routines into practice. By using tailored ways to deal with insomnia and restlessness, we can conquer sleep issues and reach our full potential with the aim of the greatest accomplishment.

CHAPTER NINE

Maintaining the Mind and Body

In our pursuit of better focus, fewer outside distractions, and success, we sometimes neglect two essential foundations of health, which are exercise and proper diet. These factors have a significant impact on our ability to think clearly, operate mentally, and be productive in general. We can reach our greatest potential and succeed in our endeavors by being aware of how nutrition affects brain function, integrating exercise into our daily schedules, and cultivating the mind-body connection.

Five Essential Guidelines for Evaluating Dietary Effects on Brain Function

Think of your brain as a highly efficient engine. It needs the proper fuel to run as well as any other engine. Our diets have a direct impact on our mental capacities and overall state of health. Here are five essential ideas to think about:

1. Balanced Nutrition: Vital nutrients for brain function can be obtained from a diet rich in fruits, vegetables, whole grains, lean meats, and healthy fats. Nuts and fish such as salmon are good sources of omega-3 fatty acids, which are especially good for mental wellness.

2. Hydration: Dehydration can affect focus and mental function negatively. Maintain proper hydration all through the day by consuming natural fruit juices, herbal teas, and plenty of water.

3. Mindful Eating: Use mindful eating techniques to better recognize hunger signals, facilitate better digestion, and avoid overindulging. While eating, chew food carefully, enjoy every bite, and keep yourself from becoming distracted.

4. Restrict Sugar and Processed Food Intake: Consuming too much sugar and processed food can cause emotional imbalance, energy drops, and mental numbness. Whenever feasible, choose whole food sources and healthy sweeteners.

5. Supplements: To promote brain health, take into account vitamins B, D, and C along with minerals such as magnesium and zinc, with the advice of a healthcare provider.

Four Strategies for Including Movement in Your Everyday Life

Not only is physical activity good for our bodies, but it also has a significant positive effect on mental health and performance. These four ideas will help you include physical activity in your everyday life:

1. Consistent Exercise: Try to get a minimum of thirty minutes of moderate to intense exercise most days of the week. Exercises like yoga, dancing, weight training, brisk walking, and jogging help improve mood, lower stress levels, and improve focus.

2. Recesses and Stretching: Whenever possible, take a pause from sedentary lifestyles like using electronics or working at a desk. To refresh your mind, take advantage of these moments to stretch, move about, or perform brief physical activities.

3. Open-air Duration: Spend as much time as you can in the great outdoors. Taking walks in the outdoors, gardening, or just taking in the natural light may all lift your spirits and foster creativity.

4. Mindful Movement: Pay attention to your breath, your body's feelings, and the here and now when you exercise to cultivate awareness. This strengthens the advantages of physical activity and fosters a closer mind-body connection.

Four Strategies for Developing a Robust Mind-Body Connection

The body and mind are deeply influenced by one another and are closely intertwined. Developing a robust mind-body connection can help you focus better, feel less stressed, and be more resilient in general. Here are four strategies to develop a robust mind-body connection:

1. Mindfulness Practices: Include yoga, deep breathing techniques, or mindfulness meditation in your everyday practice. These techniques encourage calmness, mental clarity, and emotional well-being.

2. Quality Sleep: To promote mood control, information retention, and brain function, give priority to sound sleep. Aspire to get between seven to nine hours of sleep every night, establish a relaxing nighttime ritual, and improve your sleeping environment.

3. Stress Control: Create efficient stress-reduction plans that include time management, setting priorities, practicing relaxation techniques, and reaching out to others for assistance. Prolonged stress can harm one's general health and mental function.

4. Comprehensive Well-Being: Adopt an overall approach to wellness by looking for meaning and purpose in everyday activities, cultivating relationships, and engaging in hobbies and gratitude exercises. Mental toughness and focus are enhanced by a fulfilling existence.

By endeavoring to utilize the truth of exercise, diet, and the mind-body connection, you may maximize the benefits of dopamine detox to reduce distractions, improve focus, and accomplish your objectives with purpose and precision. it's important for you to acknowledge the fact that long-term success and comfort are built on a healthy body and mind.

CHAPTER TEN

Conquering the Three Main Obstacles on the Path to Dopamine Detox

There will inevitably be obstacles on the path to dopamine detox that will try your perseverance and willpower. In order to reduce distractions, increase focus, and ultimately achieve success, it is essential to deal with setbacks and relapses, control cravings and enticements, and develop resilience.

1. Managing Relapses and Setbacks: During the dopamine detox process, relapses and setbacks are frequent occurrences. It's critical to realize that these are chances for development and education instead of failures. The following five techniques will assist you in overcoming setbacks and relapses:

a. Self-Compassion: Show yourself kindness when facing obstacles. Recognize that everyone has obstacles to overcome and that making mistakes is normal. Stay away from self-criticism and concentrate on the lessons you can take away from the event.

b. Ponder and Examine: Give it some thought as to what caused the backslide or setback. Was it a specific stressor, emotional condition, or trigger? By identifying the underlying reason, you may create preventative measures to avoid reoccurring problems.

c. Modify Your Goals: If your original objectives were very lofty or unrealistic, think about lowering them to a more manageable level. In order to prevent feeling defeated, break major ambitions down into smaller, more feasible steps.

d. Seek Support: If you need inspiration or direction, don't be afraid to get in touch with friends, family, or a support group. Talking about your experiences with like-minded people can yield insightful and inspiring discussions.

e. Remain Persistent: Let failures strengthen your resolve by using them as fuel. Recall that persistence is essential for enduring success and that development is not always a straight course.

2. Dealing with Cravings and Temptations: If you don't deal with cravings and temptations well, they can ruin your plans to go through a dopamine detox. The following five techniques can assist you in overcoming temptations and cravings:

a. Determine Triggers: Acknowledge the circumstances, feelings, or surroundings that set off cravings. Once these triggers have been detected, you can create proactive coping mechanisms or avoidance tactics.

b. Distract Yourself: Take part in pursuits that take your mind off of your cravings. Positive mental occupations include mindfulness exercises, physical activity, hobbies, and social interactions with encouraging people.

c. Engage in Mindfulness Practice: Recognize your thoughts and desires without passing judgment on them hastily. You can maintain your composure and sense of control by practicing mindfulness exercises like systematic muscle relaxation, deep breathing, and meditation.

d. Healthier Substitutions: Opt for healthier substitutes in place of bad routines or cravings. For instance, choose fruits or nuts in place of sweet snacks if you're craving them. Look for alternatives that satisfy you just as much without jeopardizing your dopamine detoxification objectives.

e. Establish a Supportive Environment: Assemble a group of individuals who value and support your goals. To lessen enticement, eliminate or limit your physical environment's triggers and temptations.

3. Developing Resilience: Sustaining enduring dopamine detoxification success requires developing resilience. Being resilient makes it possible for you to overcome obstacles, recover from setbacks, and successfully adjust to changes. Here are five strategies for developing resilience:

a. Develop Positivity: Pay attention to the good parts of your path and acknowledge your little accomplishments along the route. To change your perspective and adopt an optimistic and resilient outlook, start a thankfulness practice.

b. Realistic Expectations: Steer clear of fear of imperfection and give yourself reasonable hope. Recognize that failures are a normal part of development and that improvement requires time and struggle.

c. Gain Wisdom from Adversity: Rather than brooding over mistakes, look for ways to improve. Think back on the lessons you've gained from your experiences and the best way to utilize them on the path to dopamine detoxification.

d. Create Coping Strategies: Assemble a toolkit of coping mechanisms, including tactics for regulating emotions, and problem-solving abilities, and encouraging personal development. These techniques will assist you in handling challenging circumstances with fortitude.

e. Seek Balance: Give self-care, such as getting enough sleep, eating a healthy diet, exercising, and relaxing, a top priority. In order to avoid weariness and preserve general comfort, strike a balance between work and rest time.

You may conquer obstacles, control cravings, and develop resilience by putting these tactics into practice as you set off for a dopamine detox that will reduce distractions, increase focus, and ultimately lead to success. Never forget that every action you do, regardless of how tiny, puts you one further step toward your objectives.

CHAPTER ELEVEN

How to Include Dopamine Detox in Your Lifestyle in Three Easy Steps

You have made a great choice for deciding to start a dopamine detoxification program. By making this move, you're starting down the path to decreased distractions, increased attention, and eventually reaching your objectives. In this chapter, we'll explore the three easy steps to incorporating dopamine detox into your lifestyle. They include incorporating dopamine detox activities into your everyday routine, embracing lifelong learning and development, and celebrating your victories in the process.

1. Incorporating Dopamine Detox Activities into your Everyday Routine: Developing a balanced everyday routine is the first step for effective dopamine detoxification. To begin, decide what your top priorities are and set up certain time slots for work, education, exercise, and leisure. Here are five essential suggestions for establishing a well-balanced routine:

a. Establish Clear Objectives: Make sure that every day, week, and month has definite, attainable goals. You'll be able to remain energized and focused with this precision.

b. Prioritize Your chores: Make sure you focus on the things that really matter by using strategies such as Eisenhower's Urgent/Important concept to differentiate between important and urgent chores.

c. Time Blocking: Set aside specified periods of time for various tasks to reduce multitasking and improve focus.

d. Mindful Breaks: Take brief pauses during work to refuel your energy and avert exhaustion. Take part in relaxing exercises like stretching, deep breathing, or taking a quick stroll outside.

e. Consistency: Adhere to your regimen regularly, making necessary adjustments in light of your development and impact.

You may foster a favorable environment for your dopamine detox endeavor by implementing a balanced routine, which will help you efficiently control distractions and maximize your performance.

2. Constant Learning and Development: Embracing lifelong education and personal development is essential to dopamine detoxification. Developing a curious mentality and looking for learning opportunities can improve your general success, creativity, and mental capacities. The following five strategies can help you make lifelong education a part of your routine:

a. Read Frequently: Find time to read books, articles, or academic textbooks about topics relevant to your interests and career advancement. Think about a variety of subjects to extend your thinking.

b. Enhancement of Skills: List the abilities you wish to develop or get, such as time optimization, eloquence, or programming. To improve these abilities, sign up for workshops, digital lectures, or courses.

c. Reflective Practice: Give your experiences, difficulties, and knowledge some thought. Writing in a journal or engaging in meditation might help one become more self-aware and mature.

d. Ask for Opinion: Ask mentors, colleagues, or subject-matter experts for their opinions. You can strengthen your techniques and uncover areas that need development with the use of constructive comments.

e. Networking: Meet people who share your interests and share ideas by participating in seminars, business conferences, or professional associations.

You may improve your skills and gain valuable experiences and wisdom to thrive with your dopamine detox endeavor by welcoming ongoing education and development.

3. Honoring Significant Breakthroughs and Achievements: As your dopamine detox progresses and you witness a significant breakthrough, it's critical to recognize and commemorate your efforts and accomplishments. Festivities are strong motivators that uplift spirits and reinforce good deeds. Here are four ideas for commemorating breakthroughs and successes:

a. Recognize Progress: Evaluate your development on a consistent basis and acknowledge minor accomplishments during the journey. Acknowledge the work you've done and the breakthroughs you've accomplished.

b. Reward System: Create a system whereby you indulge yourself in something fun or exceptional when you accomplish important goals. This may be a day off to rest, your favorite dish, or a little shopping you've had your eye on.

c. Share Your Success: Inform loved ones, friends, and encouraging groups about your accomplishments. Rejoicing with others improves your interpersonal relationships while also fostering a feeling of success.

d. Evaluate and Make New Objectives: Give yourself some time to consider your accomplishments, lessons learned, and personal development. Make use of this knowledge to continue your quest for private and business growth by setting new objectives.

You may maintain motivation to go after your goals, build positive habits, and increase your confidence by acknowledging and commemorating your accomplishments.

Finally, adopting dopamine detoxification techniques into your life can be a life-changing experience that increases success, performance, and focus. You can embark on this pursuit with resilience and tenacity if you establish a well-balanced routine, accept life's ongoing learning and development, and recognize and celebrate your successes along the way. It's important for you to acknowledge the fact that self-analysis and consistency are essential elements of long-term development. Accept the journey, remain dedicated to your objectives, and relish the fruits of a life well-thought-out and meaningful.

CONCLUSION

As we come to the end of our dopamine detox adventure, we have gained a wealth of knowledge on how to design a life with fewer distractions, more focus, and ultimate success. We have explored the complex mechanisms of the brain's reward system in this book, learning how dopamine affects our everyday decisions and behaviors.

To summarize the main ideas, we started by realizing how commonplace distractions are in the present times, from social media notifications to the never-ending stream of information clamoring for our attention. We discovered that dopamine can be an ambidextrous weapon, deceiving us into bad behaviors that impede our progress even while it is necessary for motivation and enjoyment.

With this knowledge in hand, we set off on a detoxification adventure, picking up useful techniques to cut down on dopamine-producing triggers and get our focus back. We looked at the effectiveness of conscious goal-setting, habit reformation, and mindfulness practices as strategies to resist the pull of rapid satisfaction.

The central theme of our investigation has been liberation. We are capable of rewiring our behaviors, reshaping our neurological pathways, and regaining control over our focus. We can realize our deepest desires and maximize our potential by living a life that is conscious of the merits and demerits of the dopamine effect.

As this book draws to an end, I urge you to keep going forward on your path of dopamine detox with dedication and resolve. A changed perspective is not something that can be established with ease, as major achievements take time. Honor each little accomplishment, take lessons from failures, and remain dedicated to the development path.

Never forget that you have the ability to control your own fate. Using the dopamine detox concept to your advantage will help you achieve great focus, worthwhile goals, and long-lasting success in addition to minimizing distractions. Continue onward and do not look back as you journey on the path of dopamine detox, because there is a great light at the end of the dark tunnel of mastering dopamine detoxification.

ABOUT THE AUTHOR

James Edwards was born on May 16th, 1974. He suffered from schizophrenia in the year 1998, which threatened to ruin his mental health. It happened that when James Edwards was miraculously healed of his mental sickness in the year 2012, he decided to serve mankind with his mental prowess. He does rigorous research on relevant subject matters and documents his discoveries in the form of concise and clear short nonfiction books.

"FINANCIAL LITERACY FOR TEENS AND YOUNG ADULTS" is one of his popular books. Other books include "UNDERSTANDING MEDICAL TERMINOLOGY BY MASTERING PREFIX AND SUFFIX," "LOWER CHOLESTEROL NATURALLY," and "A SHORT DESCRIPTION OF THE SECRET OF RELIEVING PAIN BY TRAINING YOUR NERVOUS SYSTEM DIFFERENTLY." He is a prolific author of plenty of short nonfiction books. Every word James writes is infused with his genuine desire to positively impact every reader's life and his passion for personal progress.

Start reading James Edwards's books now to begin your road toward a more purposeful and happy existence.

You can discover his other useful and highly interesting short books by visiting his author central page here: https://www.amazon.com/author/jamesedwards1974

www.ingramcontent.com/pod-product-compliance
Lightning Source LLC
Chambersburg PA
CBHW070949220526
45471CB00007B/2955